THINGS
I SHOULD'VE TOLD
MY MOMMA

I Finally,Let my Guards Down

Written By

Daphne Johnson

CONTENTS

Introduction

I promised myself that I would never talk about what happened. It was just too embarrassing and painful. I was all set and ready to take it to my grave. I honestly thought I was doing great. It didn't drive me to drugs or alcohol so hell I was winning, and no one would ever know what happened! My secret was safe! But baby was I wrong. I was so wrong, it started showing up in my life and God kept trying to get my attention, but I refused to listen until it just took a toll on me about two and half years ago.

God had been trying to get my attention for years and I kept pushing it away and hiding from it. I mean God removed everyone from my life and just left me with me to think and deal with my own trauma. Here I am running around and giving people great advice, telling them how special they are. You have to keep fighting, you got kids, naw, God wants you to be happy, God has something great in store for you. I was always on the phone praying with friends for hours and was being there for everybody. I was making everyone's problems my own and was always available for everyone – showing up for everyone except for myself.

I was always telling everyone they are worthy of a great relationship, but not seeing it for myself. Being the light at the end of everyone's dark tunnel but could not be my own light. It was such a heavy burden to carry all these years by myself. But now, I have the courage to speak up! And speak out! My prayer is that this book will help someone that is scared and silent or those who feel they are not worthy of love.

Dedication

This book is dedicated to my beautiful mom, grandma, kids, sisters, nieces, nephews, family and friends. Mama, there was so much I wish I had the courage to tell you, but I just couldn't add more to your suffering. Thanks for introducing us to God at a young age because God, faith, you, grandma and my sisters got me through my challenges. Without that, I don't think I would have made it this far. I love you just the same way you loved us all.

Grandma, you have literally been my everything. I wish I could have told you what was going on. But we all know how that would have ended and we need you here with us. I love you so much.

To my four beautiful children; Naquasha Johnson (youngest sister), Daphne' Johnson (still born), Daniya Johnson and Dajuan Johnson. Without you all, I would have never had the courage to write this book. I love you guys beyond what words or actions can say or show. Thank you guys for always loving me unconditionally. I know it wasn't easy. I know I was, and I am very overprotective of you all. But y'all could never really understand why. Hopefully, this gives you guys just a little understanding. And always know my famous line; "I will rock that orange jumpsuit proudly if someone ever tries one of y'all." Love always Mom, Taye.

To all six of my beautiful, talented, smart, educated and God-fearing sisters. I love you guys with all my heart. We might have our differences because we all have been through so much. We might argue and cuss each other out. But I know without a doubt if I need you guys, y'all will be there. Lasonya, Kenisha. Waukesha, Latora, Daisha, and Naquasha. I hope this book brings some kind of understanding of me. Love y'all little and big sisters.

To all my nieces and nephews, y'all already know auntie Taye loves you guys. Marquis, Shaquisha, Tajuan, Oshaye, Keondae, Juanita, Amare, Ronnie Jr, Carter, Carson, Ariya, Keajah, Kanita, Daron, Dajah, Lauren, Addison, Amir, and Toni. Please remember to keep God first in anything y'all do and anything is possible with God and faith. Never let anyone steal your voice and silence you. Speak up and speak out! Love you all, auntie Taye.

To my true friends that have had to deal with me over the years. I take full responsibility for the wrongs I have done, and I know some of you tried hard to understand me and love me regardless, but at the time, I was not capable of accepting love. I could not see how people that were not related to me could love me like family because, in my world, I was hurt by people that were supposed to be family. So, I unknowingly kept my guards up at all times. But I am forever grateful that God lent you all to me to help me figure this thing out. It hasn't been easy but thanks for saying girl, I love you but I'm going to give you your space in that space. I have figured myself out, learned my purpose and learned to shine my light. Much love and respect to you all.

Wasn't Supposed to Make it "My Birth"

I was born to the beautiful, loving and caring Juanita Johnson and Jerome Huges on September 21, 1977, at Mount Sini Hospital. I'm the second oldest of six girls. When I was born, I had a rough start. I was premature. I came when my mom was about six months. My mom said I was so small, I weighed only three pounds. Back then, it was not the way things are now. The doctors had given up on me. They thought I wasn't going to make it. My mom said the doctors had given up on me and rolled me to the side to die! But all of a sudden, my mom said I started sucking my thumb.

The doctor saw that and came running saying I was showing signs that I was hungry. They got me and tube-fed me. I stayed in the hospital for a while. My mom said I was covered head to toe with needles and tubes. She said I was so small I looked like a little wet rat. My grandma always told me this story with so much pride as to how my mama came to that hospital every day on the bus to see me and if you are from Chicago, you know how the fall weather was in September 1977.

She said I was so small; you could hold me in one hand. One day she was bathing me, and my grandma came into the bathroom and said Nita where's the baby? She lifted me in the palm of her hand with that beautiful smile she had and gently said, mama right here. My mama used to tell us this story with so much pride and joy.

So, at a young age, I knew God was real. The doctors had given up and rolled me to the side to die. But I had a praying Mother. And God answered her prayers and said I give you life!!!!!!!!

Erie Street
(Emma Building)
Nash Elementary School

I had to be like seven or eight years old when it all started. At the time, we were staying in Emma building. My mom would take us down south to see her father. They were some of the best times of my life. Her father was more like a father to us. As with many of us, he had each grandchild spoiled in his own little way. I honestly do not remember my granddaddy ever telling one of us no. I would say growing up, he was the closest thing to a father I had. I remember him having that beautiful smile like my momma.

Down there, we visited our great grandma, aunts, uncle, and cousins. Most of our family stayed in the south. I knew I was safe and felt unconditional love there. They used to be so excited about "our cousin from Chicago here." They were genuinely happy to see us and made us all feel at home. Even though we were all so excited to see our family, I think I can say my sisters and I all agree on a couple of things: we hated how hot it was the mosquitoes and the brown water. I remember the first time someone ran us some bath water and said take a bath. My sisters and I looked at the water and said, we are not ready to take a bath in that dirty water.

The mosquito bites were so bad, when we got back, we had to go to Dr. LaSalle's office on Chicago Ave. and get clammy lotion. But one of my sisters really had a bad reaction to the bites. She would swell up and have to take medication by mouth too.

One night, my mom was getting ready for company to come over for a card game. The living room, dining room and one bedroom was in the front, my mom was in the front of the house. Our bedroom was at the back by the kitchen and bathroom. So, she was getting ready for her guest, and we were in our room. One thing my mom didn't play about was kids sitting around in a grown-up business. We knew when she had company, they were talking to go to our room. She had us take our baths and put on our pajamas. He came in playing like he was helping me put the medication on.

He started rubbing up my legs, my buttocks and then inserted his finger in me. I felt so confused, scared, embarrassed and ashamed. I didn't know what to do. As the tears rolled from my eyes, he said, you better not tell anybody! This was a grown-ass nasty man doing this. He is supposed to be like family. I can't remember who walked into the room at that point. He jumped and said that I had wasted the lotion everywhere and he was helping me to clean it up. I was just an eight-year-old kid who was very shy. I didn't know what to do or say as I lay there in that top bunk bed. I was so confused and scared.

I can remember my mom saying as clear as day, you always burn yourself when you iron. You're gonna have to stop ironing. I couldn't tell her it helped me release some of my pain and confusion. You need to be careful she would say. One time my gown got stuck to my burn He played like he was trying to help me get it off. Once again, he took advantage of the situation and when someone walked in, he said he was helping me.

My mama's best friend stayed across the street and her best friend's parents stayed a building over. Next door to us was where her best friend's sisters lived, and these were people my mom had known for a while. She looked at them as family and her best friend's sisters hung out with my oldest sister. One of her best friend's sister or her friend who own the building used to always get my sister (that was right under me) they used to take her with them all the time. They were like our second family. My oldest sister used to be at her dad's house.

But I do believe he felt I had no one and that was why he was doing what he was doing. As time went on, I just withdrew more and stayed to myself. I remember we had moved from Erie and my mom had come back to drop some Avon off. We pull up and my mom had a church song on the car radio. I was just sitting in the back of the car clapping and rocking to the song. I will never forget when they started laughing and I heard someone say, look at her ass, she is going to be sanctified and it didn't make it any better. I used to love to wear skirts and dresses.

But I didn't care. I just kept clapping and rocking because I knew what I was praying for, and only if they knew what God and I knew.

I had some of my best and worst times in Erie. My Grandma stayed in Gray Indiana. My Granddad stayed down south, and all my mom's aunts, uncles and cousins stayed out of town. My mom's brother, his wife and kids stayed with us. One of the best memories I cherish was going to Helping Hand M.B Church and listening to Rev. Kelly and Pastor Woolridge. I enjoyed going to church on Sunday morning to hear the choir. It was this little lady dress to a T! Baby!!! My siblings and I used to be so excited when she sang.

This little lady with this big voice was directing the choir and singing at the same time. One of my funniest childhood memories was when my siblings and I took turns to stand on a stool, put on a big robe and mimic her. We couldn't sing very well but you better believe we were in every kid's choir as long as I can remember. So even though I was going through some of the darkest times of my life, God was always shinning his light here and there to let me know he was still with me.

Walton Days

My mom bought a two-flat building on Walton and Keeler. I was so proud of her. She did that! All the hard work keeping her credit in good standards and all the doubles and savings had paid off. Do you know how big it was for a woman to do that in the '80s? That mortgage statement read, Juanita Johnson and Juanita Johnson only. But did she really know what she sacrificed to give her kids a better life?

Now don't get me wrong, she was with him for a while. A lot of people saw him in the house and thought he was doing it. He helped her out, but we saw our mom put in the hard work, the doubles, (sometimes four and five times a week) working for two different nursing homes and going to Triton College to get her GED. Going back to Triton to be a certified CNA after going back to sign up for a program to be a teacher assistant for Chicago public school. She was so busy going to school, working, selling Avon for extra income to raise her girls, and making sure everyone stayed on track (one thing she didn't play about was education.) that it created the space for the devil to sneak in.

I loved where we moved to, but I just hated all the bad things that happened in that building. But I will say we met some amazing people over there. Our mom's brother stayed on the second floor with his wife and kids. We were really a close family, and his kids were like our siblings. Everyone knew my mom loved her nieces, nephews and grandkids as if they were her own. We stayed on the first floor and the basement. My mom had a cut-out put in the kitchen floor that leads to the basement. It was an open area and on the other side was the washer and dryer. Coming towards the front of the basement was a bathroom and coming through a kitchen was a big bedroom and that's where my sisters and I slept. The living room was at the front by the basement door.

My mom was strict; she was one of them old school parents and didn't play about disrespect in any way. If she comes home and finds out someone was fighting, you best believe she was ready to whip your ass and after that, y'all will sit there and hold hands. Catch her on a bad day and you will receive punishment too. She always used to say, "when I'm dead and gone, y'all are only going to have each other." But she also had this lovely and sweet side, which is the biggest heart to this day. I still haven't met anyone like her. Always helping people and never complaining. Her faith was unmatched. A lot of people didn't know our mother was a jokester. One of my favorite memories of her was when her my sister and I were all sitting in one room, just laughing, talking and playing the game Super Mario was a family favorite and our mom use to be yelling screaming and jumping like the characters in the game can actually get her, we used to laugh so hard at her.

As we started getting older, we started telling her how she tries to help everyone and if she needed them, they wouldn't do the same for her. She always replied with that beautiful smile that she was not worried because God was going to bless her! Man: my mom's faith is something I admired. When we moved to Walton, we were the kids that once the streetlights came on, we had to come into the house. We went to church every Sunday and observe big Sunday dinners every Sunday. She combs our hair every morning before school and when something went wrong, there will be family meetings.

My mom cooked a full dinner every day. Even if she worked or had to do a double, she would come home, cook, make us do homework, lay our school clothes for the next day and go back to work. One of my favorite memories of her was going to the store and going through the different patterns so she could make our summer clothes. Summer came and she would pull her sewing machine out and make most of our summer clothes. My mom made the best two-piece short sets and the best summer dress.

Though she did all this and was worried about the outside world hurting us, she was not aware of the danger in her own home. She was sleeping with the devil, had kids by him and let his offspring move in; he was no better than his father.

Every summer, we would go down south to see our family for summer vacation for a week. We were that family that went to the zoo every summer, museum, bowling, Kiddie Land, Skating rink, we went to the beach, and also to the lakefront most weekends because he loved to go fishing. If only I had the courage to run up behind him and push him into the lake, all my problems would have been resolved. But how would I be able to face my sisters and tell them I killed their dad? We went to the big Christmas party downtown. We had the game systems Atari and Nintendo. My mom signed us up in the off-the-street club, etc.

She was always doing something. This woman learned how to do Jerry curls when everyone started wearing them. Everyone in our house had curls. She was always trying to make life better for us. Lord, but the one thing she couldn't do was protect me from what was in our home. She didn't know she was with the devil himself. I wanted to tell her so badly, but these words were stuck in my head, that he would kill her. I couldn't take a chance, so I just kept quiet.

As we got older, we were allowed to go to three people's houses, one friend's house which was my sister's best friend and, in their backyard. Another stayed a house away from us and another across the street which was our oldest sister's friend, and we were friends with her younger sister. My mom's favorite line was that they can spend the night over at our house. It's so weird how hard my mother tried to keep us safe from the outside danger of the world not knowing of the danger in our own home. She was sleeping with the devil. When someone spends the night, he wouldn't try anything.

He thought he was so clever; he did not draw attention to himself. I'm forever grateful to that friend that would stay over or those we were able to spend the night at that one friend house they also had a big family too they family was always nice and so welcoming. Sometimes friends would also stand at the basement bars with us because our Mama was at work, and we could not come outside, or we were on punishment. I also appreciate the friends that just stopped by and stood on the porch with us or in the hallway because I was safe in those moments. The only issue was having to walk back past him to get into the house.

Whenever we were in the hallway or on the porch talking with friends, he would be by the window or at the door listening. When he hears or sees us coming, he would run and sit back on the couch like he was just watching TV. We would always see the blinds moving. I truly believe he was sneaking around and trying to make sure I did not tell anyone what was going on. I'm forever grateful for the angels that God had placed in my life, the ones who didn't let someone's attitude turn them away. Because whenever people came around, he would try so hard to be mean to them, just to scare them away and stop them from coming around.

The basement door had bars on them because once again he lied and told my mom someone tried to break into the house, so they put bars on the basement door and windows. He was so good at what he was doing that he had everyone fooled!!!!! He would send my sisters to the store and make me stay. Once they were gone, he would rape me. He always said the same thing as he finished; "if you tell anyone, I will kill your momma." As I started to fight back, he would say if you keep it up, I'm going to do it to your sisters. Lord knows I wanted to say something so badly. I wanted to tell my mama so badly, but I could not risk it.

And I have to be honest with myself; I was terrified, embarrassed, and ashamed. I allowed this to go on. It was my fault. I wish I had put aside the fact that he was my sibling's father and called the police or try to kill him myself. But I just knew if I tried, he would kill my mom or if I killed him, I would go to jail. If I said something, my mama would have gotten into trouble, or they would have taken us from her. I couldn't take the chance. My brain was always running and thinking of ways to escape this hell. I lived in fear, shame and embarrassment all the time.

This man was so low down that whenever we were watching the TV, he would change the channel to something else if we were enjoying a program just to be spiteful. So, what I learned to do was program myself to be able to watch anything no matter what it was. To this day, my sisters will say Taye watches anything. I was so scared it was going to happen again if I go to sleep at night that I would go to bed without sleeping off. I would stay up late hoping, wishing and praying this would stop. Hoping that they would just leave me the fuck alone.

I remember having this dark-skinned teacher that wore big glasses. At Piccolo Elementary, I was in her class. I think I was in third or fourth grade and it was time for report card pick up. My mom went in to talk to her because I had failed some classes. So, my mom was up there trying to find out what was going on. I knew why I was falling, and it was because I was not sleeping at night. I was scared to go to sleep because I knew he was going to come in. So, I stayed up and when I got to school, Lord knows I tried my best to stay awake in class, but I just couldn't. At least I knew I was safe in class. I was mad at this teacher for a long time because she stood there and told my mom there wasn't anything wrong with Daphne. She's just lazy!!! I was so mad at her for a long time. I wanted to tell her so bad; lady, look here I can't sleep at night because my home is not safe. I tried my best to stay awake.

Often, teachers write students off for being lazy but not all students are lazy. Some are just going through some heavy stuff. Teachers sometimes need to look a little closer. I was standing there screaming within me like, really? Lazy lady! LAZY!!!!!! If you knew what I was up against at home, maybe you would reconsider your choice of words. Needless to say, I failed, not because I was lazy but because I wasn't sleeping at night and since I was not sleeping at night, I couldn't focus on schoolwork because I would be so sleepy. The most embarrassing thing ever. So, at this point, I was dealing with molestation, rape, failure and my self-esteem was even lower now. I need to remind you that I was not a bad student just very quiet and standoffish.

I wanted to tell my mom so badly that they were messing with me, but I was just too scared to tell. I was too ashamed and thought it was my fault. I watched my momma take off work and attend all kinds of meetings trying to figure out what was wrong with me. Her thinking was that I was a premature baby, and they did tell her I might have some problems. She was thinking that's what was going on. Never in a million years would she have thought that what was going on.

My mom would be at work, and I'll be called upstairs. He would say, can you do me a favor and I said yes. This was before I knew what he was going to do, and he would just take what he wants. So, after that first time, he asked again, "you want to do me a favor?" I would say no, it's not like that would help. At this point, I was just feeling helpless, and I knew that no matter what I did it wasn't going to stop.

How can someone so evil have so many people fooled to think that he was a good guy? But seventh and eighth grade were cool, and we still stayed on the 4200 block of Walton while a friend of mine stayed on the 4300 block of Walton. My sister went out with her older cousin, and she was in my sister's classroom. I used to go down there with her, and we were so close that we talked about everything for hours, but I still could not say anything since the shame and embarrassment crept right in. I couldn't dare bring myself to tell her what was going on at home. I felt like it was my fault! Lord knows I wanted to tell her, but I just couldn't. If I told her, what would happen? Would my sisters be mad if I got our family into trouble? Would my grandma try to kill them and go to jail? Would they take us from my mom? Would they split my sisters and me up? I couldn't dare bring that type of shame and embarrassment to my family.

I had some great elementary friends. Z is another person that used to just pop up at my house and we would stand in the hallway or the porch and talk for hours. Z was one of the nicest souls you could ever meet. She had such a beautiful smile and a soft caring voice, but I still could not open up and tell her. How do you tell someone something like that?

My oldest sister had some really cool friends. They didn't mind me tagging along with my older sister. One friend, in particular, stayed around the corner from us. We used to visit her all the time and my sister would be in the front talking. At such times, I found a moment of peace and was able to get some sleep. Her bed was against the wall with all of these stuffed animals, and I would cuddle up with them and go to sleep. I wanted to say something so bad, but I didn't want to get my mom into trouble.

I kept telling myself, tell!!!!!!! This is your chance to get some help because her father is a Chicago police officer. He can help. Or can he? Did I really want to gamble with my mom's life? How would my sisters feel about me telling? Would they split us up? Should I take a chance?!!!! I kept having an out-of-body experience of me telling but I just could not say it out loud. When I even thought about it, I would instantly feel sick, ashamed, nasty, embarrassed and responsible for letting this happen to me. I honestly could not believe that this was happening. How can one be this wicked? How can you be with my mom for years, have kids by her and every chance you got you raped her child over and over again, how?

The Apple Doesn't Fall Too Far from the Tree

His son was staying with us for the summer and caught me coming down the basement stairs. He said I know what my dad is doing to you. I stopped and was frozen in fear and as scared as I was, I honestly thought he was going to help me or get me some help. He walked up to me as if he was going to tell me something. He whispered in my ear, "I know what my dad is doing to you" I stood there scared to death and I thought that everyone was going to know about it. I was shocked and couldn't believe he knew what was going on. For a second, I thought he was going to get me some help with his low-down dirty dog of a father.

He pulled a zip lock bag out and threw me down and before I knew what was going on, he was on top of me. I felt the zip lock bag stretching my insides. I was so scared and in disbelief as he put his hands over my mouth and just handled his business. What the fuck is going on? Did his father train him? You're supposed to be my brother. You're supposed to protect me. How can you? Now, who do I trust? At that moment I made up my mind.

Fuck it! You can't trust anyone. This is the time I just got really angry, and I think my mouth got really reckless, so I built an invisible cement wall around me. My guards were up, and they weren't coming down for anyone, family or friends. I didn't trust anyone, boy or girl, woman or man. I walked around scared all the time, at school, outside the store or even when someone would just speak to me. I was no longer comfortable whenever people enter into my personal space and if they crossed the line, it always made me feel uncomfortable. I would instantly tense up and go into fight mode.

That was one of the most uncomfortable, scariest things to have to deal with. I used to be so happy when he was at work and his son went to visit his mom for the weekend. I was so mad and scared when his son moved in with us. Now I was trying to escape both of them. It just made me withdraw more and more. I was trying to stay away from him and didn't want to be left alone with them. It was like I couldn't win this battle in any way. So, I just learned that you can't trust anyone and kept my guards up at all times. I ended up graduating 8th grade, but I felt bad because I was taking some of my sister's shine. That was her moment and she worked really hard to get here and because I couldn't keep up with everything, I failed, and we ended up graduating together.

I was happy I did it, but I still felt bad. My mom had to pay double for everything, and I was like, if I didn't fail, she wouldn't have gone through all this stress. I watched her go from store to store looking for our eight-grade dress. She bought our dress, went to Dian shoe store and bought our shoes for graduation. She also got our hair and nails done all by herself because my father has never been involved in my life at all. She never said one bad word about him as things came up. She just did what she had to do, and I think at this time, my hate for my father was the strongest. This man called up here to lie and say "oh, I'm going to send you some money to help with the kids' graduation."

Needless to say, he never sent it. That just pissed me all the way off. When he called, my mom with her gentle voice said Taye, your father wants to talk to you. I was so mad. I didn't want to talk to him. I went all the way off. That's one thing my mom always let me do — express myself when it came to my father. I would do all this screaming and hollering and being mad and she would gently tell me; that is your father, and you don't have to go to hell because of him. I really didn't understand what that meant until I got older. I'm doing all this yelling for nothing and no matter what I think is wrong, I am not God.

I cannot judge him, that is between him and God. But at that young age, I couldn't wrap my mind around why she wasn't mad because she had to do everything by herself. I saw my mom go above and beyond so my sister and I would not feel left out or less than my sisters, especially when their father did things for them. As kids, they couldn't understand why she did just a little more for us. She felt they had two parents, but my sister and I didn't. We just had her. I remember one summer; my sisters went to their father's house and our father was not available. So, we went out to Gray Indian with our grandma. That made me feel so bad and embarrassed since we didn't have a father to go to. But it ended up being fun. We hung out with the kids across the street from my grandma's house and we were with our grandma. She has always been like a second parent in my eyes.

Funny fact: one day, my grandma from the south called us in for supper and said we had to eat before we went back out. She sat us at the kitchen table and gave us some hot water, cornbread and milk. My sister and I looked at each other like what the hell. And my grandma told us how to put the cornbread in the milk and eat it. We sat there and she explained that back in the days that was all they had as a meal. And how our momma has us spoiled. We sat there for some time, and we did want to go back out and play so we ate it, and it wasn't that bad after all. But that was our first and last time of having it. I remember us telling our mom and she laughed and said that used to be a meal. That's all they had back in the days y'all are bless.

Orr High School

I went to Orr High school for freshman year. That was a fun and cool year. I had met some cool people despite everything that was going on at home. High school was cool. I was really starting to find my way. One of my sisters and I went to the same high school. Our oldest sister went to Westinghouse high school. We were in the same grade because I failed a grade. That for so long bothered me and I was always so embarrassed about it. In 9th grade, my computer teacher called my mom and told her that all I do was sleep in her class. She asked my mom if I was on DRUGS!!!!! Is that how you white people think? Because someone sleeps in your class you're just going to jump to drugs.

That hurt me so bad. Once again, another teacher just assumed the worst instead of trying to ask me what was going on and why I wasn't sleeping at home. My mom was steadily trying to figure out what was wrong with me, but I was just too scared to tell her what was happening. In my head, I can see myself breaking down and telling her what was going on, but I still didn't have the courage to tell her. By this time, I think it was when I was really questioning myself. Out of all my mom's kids, I was the darkest, I was the one with the big nose, full lips, big chest and when I walked, I had a switch. Is this why they were going after me because I was the ugly one?

At the end of the school year, we were getting ready to enjoy our summer when my mom came in and said my sister and I will be going down south for the summer to stay with our favorite aunt Poochie. Poochie is my father's sister even though we have only seen my father a couple of times. We were really close to his sister when we were younger, and she stayed in Chicago. We used to go over to her house with my mom for card games, and also spend the weekend with her and her kids. She treated all of my mom's kids as if they were all her nieces. She didn't make a difference in any of my mom's kids and all of us loved poochie. She was so funny that we shared so many laughs together but never crossed the line of her being our aunt.

So, I was happy we were going down there for the summer because I knew I would be safe and it would be fun, but on the other hand I was sad we had to leave our mom, sisters and friends. The day we left; my sister dyed her hair with peroxide because that was what kids were doing at that time. She came out of the house and got into the car. My mom didn't say ONE word. I came out and she went off, you messed up that your pretty jet-black hair! Oh my God, my sisters and I laughed about that for years because the only time my mom ever cussed was when she was mad. I didn't think she would be mad because I was able to experiment with my hair. I tried everything I could to try and discourage them. Like if I cut my hair maybe they wouldn't like it and leave me alone. Boy, I was wrong! So, one week I would cut one side of my hair, the next week I'll cut the other side and the next I will cut the back off. But one thing my mom always told me was how pretty my hair was. It was so thick and jet black, it looked just like a wig.

Summer With Poochie

We made it down south for the summer at our aunt Poochie's house. Poochie always came through for us. I can honestly say her home was another safe place for me. I remember the first day at her house. I remember cleaning out a room in her house so she can give my sister and me our own space. I remember meeting the lady that stayed down the street from our aunt. They call her big momma. She sold some of the best ice cups I have ever had. I remember them introducing us to people as them Dut girls and you can see the look on some of their faces. Some accepted us and some didn't. When my aunt had to work and her oldest daughter had to work, we used to go to work with our older cousin.

We didn't care because she was one of them. Older cool cousins always made us feel loved and accepted like her mom. She worked for our father's brother who had a restaurant. I remember when we first went to work with her, she walked into the restaurant loudly as she wanted to be. She is a big ball of energy with the biggest smile and was like; Uncle Jerry, do you know who they are? The tall slim man looked at us all confused and she was like them Dut girls. Them your nieces. One thing I remember about Jerry's restaurant is our cousin who is my father's sister's son. He worked there too. He also accepted us as family. He was nice, respectful and overprotective of his younger cousins.

Boy did we have some fun. My father's sister's son, our other cousin, my sister and I can't forget those big juicy Jerry burgers. It was one of the best burgers I have ever tasted. We were introduced to the sisters that stayed down the street from my aunt, the girl that stayed behind my aunt and so many more great people. God kept some amazing people around us. Even though we were around good people, we were sad when my mom first dropped us off. But we found out that a good friend of ours from Chicago had moved down there with her grandma in a town called Rising Sun. I think it was like a 15–20-minute drive from where my aunt lives.

Our older cousin took us out and I forgot how we got her grandma's house address when we went over to see her. The moment we walked through that door; she gave us the biggest hugs with so much love. When we left, we all were so sad, so we made plans for her to come to our aunt's house. Sometimes she would come over to our aunt's house and other times we would go to hers. We spent the entire summer together. It was her, my sister and I the whole summer – we were the three musketeers.

Our family treated her like family and her family treated us like family and I can't even remember half of the stuff we used to do together. But I know we all trusted each other. We all were loyal to each other, and we told each other just about everything. As close as we were, I still couldn't tell them what was going on with me. I just knew I was safe when I was around them. Every time I would think about telling, shame, embarrassment, weakness and doubt would creep right back in. I just decided to keep it to myself.

She Left Him

My mom said she waited for him to go to work. She had a U-Haul parked down the street. He pulled off to go to work and her people pulled right after he pulled off to go to work. They loaded the u- haul and she moved down south. My mom and her friend's son rode with her to Greenwood Mississippi. My oldest sister's father's mother stayed down south. Sis Dillard is one of the nicest people you will ever meet. She treated all my mother's kids the same – just a sweet godly woman. She helped my mom get the house on Murphree Drive right around the corner from my aunt Poochie who stayed on Kay White circle.

She knew the people that were renting the house. It was a beautiful ranch-style home with two full baths and three bedrooms. So again, God kept us surrounded by good people. Our mom and Poochie signed us up in school and we attended our sophomore year down south at Amanda Elzy High School. My mom was back and forth from Mississippi to Chicago because she still worked for Northwestern Memorial Hospital with their home health department. Also, she was pregnant by that monster with my baby sister. One day, I was around the corner at my aunt Poochie's house.

My mom had gone back to Chicago, and I got into an argument with the brothers that stay across the street from my aunt. I ended up fighting them. While we were fighting, I bit my bottom lip, and my mouth was bleeding. But I was so proud of myself that I fought two boys and they barely touched me. I got up, cut through the backyard and walked proudly back to my house. I burst through the front door with my head held high. My sister looked at me and said what happened to you. I told her I got into a fight with the brothers, and I was telling her I held my own.

My sister wasn't trying to hear that. She started yelling to my other sisters, "Let's go, Taye had a fight with some boys." they all grabbed bats and sticks and we left. All I could think of was the color purple when Sophia came storming through the fields and said you told Harpo to beat me. If anyone knows about the south, you know how the houses sit up in a circle and you can just walk through the yards to get to the next one. My sister the leader, red and mad as hell was yelling, "They are boys, you don't put your hands on a girl." I was still trying to tell her I held my own as I was running up behind her and my other sisters. She wasn't trying to hear it. We got there and she walked to the front of the boys' house, "Come outside, y'all like to fight girls, come outside." We were sitting there with the bats and sticks and the next thing we know, the police came pulling up and said, y'all can take that back to Chicago.

Moving Back to Chicago (Bellwood)

So here we go back to Chicago, and we thought we were ready to go back to Walton. We were so excited thinking we were ready to see all of our friends and Boom!!!! She let her brother take over the building on Walton. Her and him had bought a house together in Bellwood to be honest. I forgot how we found out they got married. I know I just was so mad. I cannot wrap my head around it! How can she marry him? I was mad at her for marry him and then I was mad at myself for not telling her what they had done to me.

She was still working for Northwestern Memorial hospital in their home health department. So, she was able to build her schedule around ours most of the time. I went to Proviso West High School. My sister and I used to ride the bus together to school. One day, on our way to the bus stop, we saw one of our friends off Walton. She and my sister had a class together. She was staying in Bellwood with her father so every morning we would walk to the bus stop we used to stop by to get her.

In the morning, (keep in mind it's the public bus), it used to be so crowded on the bus that you would have to stand up. So here we go on the bus. Every morning I was standing up sleep knocked out on the bus. My sister used to be so embarrassed! She used to whisper to me. Taye wake up. I saw it in her face. I knew she was embarrassed. But I couldn't tell her I wasn't sleeping at night. I stayed awake all night so he would not sneak up on me. It amazes me how I could sleep on a bus full of strangers I knew nothing about but didn't feel safe enough to sleep in my own home.

Junior year was good. I meet some amazing people and as close as I was to some of them, talking them through their problems; I couldn't dare tell them what was going on with me. One of the best times we had was when we got out of school and went to her house. Even if it was just for a minute, I just have to say thank you God because you kept me covered with some amazing people all the while I was in school.

In my senior year of high school, I used to get out early. I only had four classes. If I knew anyone wasn't going to be at home and he was there, I would go to Carson in Hillside. It was right down the street from the school. I used to go there just to walk around and if I got paid, I used to shop. That store saved me plenty of days because my sister and I rode the bus to school in the morning and after school, I would walk with a friend or by myself. I remember stopping by a friend's house after school only if it was for a few minutes and felt safe.

I was so scared during my senior year, but I dared not tell my mama the truth. I had failed gym and in order to graduate I had to have four years of gym and I only had one. My mama said how the hell do you get an F in gym? I just said I did not want to mess my hair up. And she believed me because she knew how I was about my hair. Ask my sisters, they used to be so mad at me. In the summertime, it used to be 90 degrees out and I would never roll the car window down because I didn't want my hair to blow. Boy oh boy, they were so mad.

I paid for that before I graduated. I had to make them gym classes up. But I did it by the grace of God. I used to try to be the first one in the locker room or the last one out, so most people will be gone. I was scared all the time. I felt everyone was always looking at me. I felt so uncomfortable changing in that locker room and I was so uncomfortable in my own skin. If I was late to gym class or had to go downstairs when a male teacher or student walked past and it was only us in the hallway, my heart would start beating so fast and I would automatically think they were going to hurt me.

There was a teacher at Proviso West that I am forever grateful for. She was a small white dorky lady that had a bowl haircut. She really cared about her students. I had her for homeroom out of all the teachers. She took her time with her students. She gave me a test and one day, she called me to her desk and said, "There is nothing wrong with you. You just have a different way of learning, and you are overprotective of the people you care about." When she told me that, it was like okay, let's do this. You can do anything. There is nothing wrong with you!

At home, things were getting worse because, by this time, my mom had gotten really sick. She was back and forth for a while before they found out that she needed a liver transplant and was diabetic. So, my mama was sick most of the time but every day she still got up and went to work, sometimes barely able to pull herself out of the bed. Her eyes had turned yellow. I remember when she had gotten so sick to the point that she hadn't the energy to work. She asked me about doing her ponytail. To this day, if my sisters ask me to do something, they always say, "Do you feel like it? Cause momma always said you fuck something up if you don't feel like it." To this day we still laugh about that.

On her way to her patient's house, many days she had to sit in the car eating saltine crackers. She felt so sick and was vomiting all over herself. Most times, she came through the door with that embarrassed look on her face and would go straight to the bathroom to clean up. The car would smell like vomit for days. One day, while taking my sister to work, she was so sick that she hit the back of another car.

But through all that, my mom never gave up. To me, my mom was a superhero! Here is a lady with seven kids, sick on her deathbed and still got up and went to work every day. She was always pounding on us about the importance of God, school, being there for one another, how we carried ourselves and about when she was dead and gone. Still as sick as my mom was, I saw this lady help anyone she could. Every Sunday, we went to Monroe Baptist church by the corner of our house. We sat on the last row from the back.

It's funny now because we used to take up an entire row – just my mom and her kids and nope, he didn't go to church with us since he belonged to another church. He even had enough nerves to be a

Deacon!!!!!! Often, the pastor links us to that name, and I instantly got mad because that man was a rapist, and I did not want to be known as them girls. I was a Johnson and that is what I want to be called. But once again I couldn't say anything because I refused to bring my mom any more pain.

Our room was upstairs so, sometimes to keep him out, I started locking the door to sleep. If the door was locked, he couldn't get up there. I remember when my mom had to work in the summer, she would leave early and try to make it back before we woke up. Some of my sisters used to ride to work with my mom. So, they gave me an idea and I told them to start waking me up so I can go with them. When it was hot outside, my mom used to see her patients. We would go to the park across the street from her patient's building close to lake shore drive and we had so much fun at that park. When I wasn't in the car sleeping, I would be at the park, and I felt so free with no worries in the world.

How evil and low down can a person be to do this to someone that is supposed to be like your child. How can someone do this to anyone? How can I tell her that her husband, the father of her kids, has been raping me for years? How can I possibly let her know about her stepson? How, how, how the hell can I take the chance of saying something that may cause him to kill my momma? How can I hurt my sisters like that and let the world know their father is a monster? And also, that their brother was a Jr. monster. So, the abuse continued. And as I started standing up for myself, he started saying it's you or one of your sisters. I just knew I had to keep them safe from this monster.

January 1996 we finally got the page we were waiting on for months. We were getting ready for school and the hospital pager went off. My mom called them back and they told her they found a match for a liver for her. No one at school knew what was going on and no one even knew my Mama was sick. She tried her best to keep things as normal as possible for us. Even with her being sick, she would just say she was sick until she told us how sick she really was. She tried her best to protect us from all the bad stuff but if only she knew it was living in our own home.

To this day, we still laugh at my mom, the sweetest lady (going to church every Sunday) and gospel-listening woman you ever meet but don't piss her off. My mom encouraged us to get a part-time job at IHOP when they first opened on North Avenue. I was a waitress. I was very standoffish and quiet around people I did not know. And not to mention that I only made $2.55 an hour plus my tips. I was mad I had to get that job, but it was an excuse to get out of that house and we did meet some amazing people there. Every time they call me to go in, I would go. My mom got her 1st transplant in January 1996. By this time, my anger for my father was stronger. Now, how do you let a sick woman fight for her life? Two out of the seven kids are yours and you still didn't step up? But his sister did help nurse my mom back to health. Just about every day Poochie, her friend and her son would come over. Poochie had moved back to Chicago and was living in Cicero, il.

She even babysits my youngest sister when my mom started work again. To me, that's just unforgivable. One thing I will say about my mom is, she NEVER said one thing about our father, good or bad and she never even tried for child support. She just continued doing what she had to do and did not complain once. Every couple of years when he calls, she would say talk to him Taye but that just angers me so badly and my mom and his sister would often say that.

I believe with all of my heart that regardless of whatever happened between him and my mom, who was wrong and who was right; two kids came out of them being together so to make an excuse for him not being there and all the bullshit and the excuse on why he wasn't there is unacceptable to me. Does anyone know how it feels to know our father had several other kids and to know he was there for them and not us? No one can ever make that right. Why he wasn't there for us, why we weren't worthy enough to have him in our lives. He failed us and I was mad as hell!!!!

I remember my mom being in the hospital and my older sister and my sister right under me coming home after seeing my mom. For some reason, every time we came back from Rush Hospital, we used to take the wrong turn and get lost. They used to be in the front of the car trying to figure out how to get home. I would lie across the back seat and sleep, and they would complain, "Taye we're lost and you're asleep. I wanted to tell them so badly that I couldn't sleep home, but I couldn't. One thing I do know is my sisters wouldn't put me in any danger so at that time I just went to sleep because I know they would not let anything happen to me.

I think maybe my mom was down six or seven weeks after that transplant and everyone was telling her she had to take it easy cause she had major surgery. I remembered my mom saying the doctor said it was a miracle how fast she was healing. Next thing you know, she was back to working full time.

I continued working there until I graduated. The IHOP workers celebrated us like we were one of their own. I received my first pager from a nice older worker there who was always so nice to us. My sister and I always laughed at how mad I was about that job, and she would often say at least I was the hostess and I got paid minimum wage. But overall, it was a wonderful experience. I will keep on saying I truly believe God always had his angels close by to make life a little happier for me. IHOP went under new management and a new manager took over. I think she said something about my sister and me missing some days because of my mom getting her liver transplant.

The manager called us to the back booth in IHOP to get us to sign a write-up. All I know my sister said was she quit, and I said, me too. We walked out. Every time that job needed us, we always came in; we never called off. But the minute my mom got sick, they wanted to write us up. She didn't even have the decency to call us into the office, she was just going to do it on the floor. We came home and told my mom what happened, and she wasn't mad cause it was not like we had to work. I think this time she was aware she wanted to be around for us, so she made us work and was trying to teach us responsibility. That year, my sick mom that had a transplant continued raising six kids that were under 18 years with the youngest being three years old. Two of her kids even managed to graduate high school. I know if it wasn't from God, I can wholeheartedly say I didn't think I could have made it.

Value City days

Value City Department Store was opened on North Ave. I got a job there so any time they would call me to come in I would go in. I would have an escape out of that house. I started working in the children's department and my mom often came there to shop for hours. I have never seen anyone shop like her... Sears, JCPenney, etc. she would go into the stores for hours and go through each and every rack and shop for hours. It is unbelievable that one person can shop that much, Lord don't let them have a sale.

Over the years, my mom started to get sick again while waiting for her second transplant. I used to take my youngest sister to work with me. I would have her in a shopping basket while I clean the area I work in or next to the register while I rung the customer. Other associates would take her to their department and keep an eye on her for me Sometimes she used to go to the LP's office while I work. My mom was really sick, and this was my way of protecting my baby sister and making sure she was safe. I just felt that if that monster could run up on me while I was sleeping, she didn't have a chance against him.

She was getting older, and I know people at work might not understood why I always had my little sister with me but that's the reason behind my action. So again, I will tell anyone God gives you who and what you need at the time, and I will forever be grateful for the people at Value City. as new managers came in, I couldn't have my little sister up there anymore.

My momma was working on buying her own house at this time. She sat every one of us down and told us that we have to give her 50 dollars every paycheck so we can have a down payment on the house. Most of the time when I gave it to her, I would eventually get it back because she ended up buying me something. Still sick, still working on her dreams and trying to get everyone through school and by this time she had started saying if anything happens to me, my girls will always have somewhere to go. I'm going to buy a house and get myself a home daycare. We saw my mom manifest and we saw her dreams come to life.

As time went on, my oldest sister moved to Bellwood with her kids' father and my sister under me moved south with her boyfriend. I really threw myself into working any time Value City called. When my oldest sister used to work, I would go over to her apartment to watch her kids. And at that point, I could put my guards down because I knew I was safe, and her boyfriend was cool, and he never said anything about me being there all the time.

In January 1999, she bought her own house in Maywood. I was finally free!

My mom finally bought a house in Maywood as she got things in order at the Bellwood home. She let her friend stay in the Maywood house and I stayed there in the Maywood house too. It was the best feeling in the world since I can now finally get some real sleep. I didn't have to always stay on guard but by this time the damage was done. I had come to be a very quiet, standoffish person around people I didn't know. I was very reserved. I had come to think that people were always up to something. I really didn't trust anyone, I couldn't sleep with the door open, I stayed to myself and when I did that, people often mislabeled me as stick up and standoffish.

Now I will take the standoffish after years of abuse by people that are supposed to be protecting me and someone that is supposed to be family. Someone who knew what was going on and used it against you. So, damn right, I am very standoffish, and I try my best to feel a person out before I engage in any type of conservation with them. I was used to working a lot so whenever they needed me, I still went in and that is my biggest regret. Getting the house in Maywood was bittersweet because as we watched my mom do everything, she said she was going to do, we knew she was sick and was still waiting on a second liver. She said I'm buying a house, got that house and opened a home daycare. She did it while still working at Northwestern Memorial.

I am going to get foster kids and try to change their lives and she did it. She had a boy and a girl. Loved the kids as if she had given birth to them herself. When one of my youngest sisters got ready to go to college in Carbondale, this sick woman that was on death bed got into her minivan with a couple of her kids and drove my sister to school. My mom was so proud pulling up to that building and dropping my sister. I will never forget pulling up on the side of that building and bringing all my sister's stuff up all the stairs. She was so proud, but you could also see the sickness in her face and eyes, but she just pushed on through.

Preparing for my First Child and Losing Her

At the end of July 1999, my mom found out that I was pregnant. I didn't tell her, my sister's boyfriend did. To this day, I still don't know how he knew. My mom called me up the stairs and asked me. At first, I tried to deny it and my sister's boyfriend, and I started arguing and the rest is history. My mom arranged a doctor's appointment and got me the proper care. I was so happy to find out I was having a girl. Everything that Value City had for a girl I bought. I picked up diapers, wipes and toys, everything was going so well. I was so happy the closet was jam-packed with baby stuff.

January 6, 2000, started like a normal day. I was off because I had a doctor's appointment. I was so happy as I left heading to my appointment, and everything seemed to be fine until they had me hooked up to the ultrasound for 30 minutes. The doctor said Miss

Johnson, we are not getting movement from the baby. They said there was no heartbeat, so they were going to put you in labor. That night, I came back to the hospital. They hooked me up to an ultrasound machine again for like 30 minutes, still no luck. Miss Johnson, we are going to give you medication to put you in labor.

They put me in labor to have my beautiful baby girl. As she was coming out. She felt warm. The doctor took her to clean her up, wrapped her in a blanket and handed her to me. They told me I had 30 minutes with her, and she was wrapped in a blanket. This pretty brown baby girl with jet black hair, a chubby little face fully developed, ten toes, and ten fingers. But she was not breathing. She looked so peaceful like she was sleeping. They said they will let us (my sister and I) keep her for 30 minutes then they will take her away.

That 30 minutes seemed like forever. When you find out you are pregnant, you start loving that baby then People often say they don't see how people are so messed up about a stillborn baby. For me, once I found out I was pregnant I instantly fell in love with the baby that was growing inside of me. In my head, I had planned her future and how she would play with her little cousin and how my mom would watch her while I worked. My mom would have her so spoiled like she has all her other grandkids. How my mom and I would've bonded, and she would have taught me all she knew about being a mom. I pictured my mom so many times in my head sitting there holding her and just smiling.

Most people leave the hospital with a baby, I left with a white folder with a red rose on it and papers on how my baby girl will be placed for burial. The folder also contained a picture of my beautiful baby girl and the blanket she was wrapped in. Though many people will never understand even though it was only 30 minutes of holding her, it still felt like a piece of me was gone and I always wonder about the what-ifs. They gave me a picture of my baby girl and let me name her Daphne' Shanee Johnson 01-6-2000 to 01-6-2000. They told me where she was buried.

My mom made some cute obituary with Daphne's pictures and personal information. And of course, she had the pastor come and pray. I was home lying-in bed. I remember my mom being sick, but she got enough energy and came to the door to ask was I okay and if I needed anything. I lied. I said yeah, I'm okay so she slowly turned and walked away. I rolled over and tears started to roll from my eyes. I was not okay, but I couldn't dare let her know that I was in pain. I was not okay. She is still fighting for life. How can I be that selfish and add something else on her and stress her more? I was off from work for a little while. The most hurtful thing to do is get all the stuff you were buying and take it back to the store.

You really don't want to be around people because they know, and you don't want sympathy. You don't want to talk about it; it's just too painful. As I watched my nieces and nephews around her age hit different milestones in life, I really thought a lot about her. She was heavy on my mind and heart at those times. Lord knows I miss her so much and I am always thinking about how lonely she was up there all by herself. They say God will never give you more than you can handle. At this point I can't lie, I questioned Him because I wanted to know why He took my baby.

September 11, 2001 - My World came Burning Down

Still working at Value City, my mom took a turn for the worst on 09-11-2001. So many people remember it because of the attacks against New York and Washington DC. I would never forget watching the news before work as the plane flew right into the twin towers with all the chaos going on. My sister dropped me off at work and a few minutes after I got there, they said they were letting us go home because another building was hit. My sister came and got me. I will never forget walking into the house through the back door and going past the bathroom. I could see blood splash on the borders of the walls and floor everywhere. My mom had been sick for maybe two weeks just in the bed she could not eat only got up to go to the bathroom. They said my mom just started throwing up blood. My sisters and I cleaned her up and took her to Rush Hospital because that was where she had her first transplant and that was where her doctors were, and they had all her health records. They knew how to treat her. I can hear my mom clear as day; if I ever get sick, y'all should take me to Rush. They have all my information, and they know how to treat me. We were only allowed to take her to the registration desk while they walked her to the back. We were not allowed to go back due to what was going on with the terrorist attack.

So, while the world was blowing up literally, our life was also blowing up. We called our grandmother from the hospital and told her what was going on. How she made it to Chicago from Gray Indian so quickly we don't know. One thing we always talk about is how grandma made it to the hospital so quickly. All jokes aside, we called her, and it seemed like 20 minutes and my grandma came bursting through the doors with her long fur coat on, calling my mom at the top of her lungs "Nita, Nita, Nita." We told my grandma they were not letting anyone see her. We saw the fear and worry in my grandma's eyes. We did what we always do and tried to act like we weren't worried and made small talks and stupid jokes.

But deep down, we knew it had to be bad because my mom never vomited blood before. Hours went by then when we were finally able to see our mom, she was just lying there sedated. The most heartbreaking thing is watching our grandma standing over her daughter and calling her name. The nurse asked us about the scars on our mom's stomach. We said she is a transplant patient. The nurse said a transplant! She didn't tell us that! I will never forget how that lady left the room and came back with all types of nurses and doctors running in there. While looking over paperwork, they put us out of the room at that point.

We were in the waiting room talking amongst ourselves. We were wondering why she asked us why we didn't tell them she was a transplant patient when they weren't letting anyone come to the back with her due to the terrorist attack. The reason why we brought her to Rush Hospital was that that's where all her doctors worked, and her information was in the system. We were all sitting there hoping and praying a liver would come in. Someone called my sister who was in Carbondale in college to let her know it wasn't looking good. Every day my mom was in that hospital, my grandma was there. You couldn't get my grandma to leave that hospital for nothing.

We watched our grandma care for her daughter till her last days. My mother and grandma had a beautiful relationship for as long as I could remember. My mom always talked highly of her mother and father. You always hear her saying my momma and my daddy. My mom had a beautiful relationship with her parents. Lord, I can only pray that my sisters and I will have the kind of love, dedication and relationships my mom had with grandma and grandpa. They used to talk on the phone for hours, go shopping together, and pray together.

Sometimes our grandma will be in church, and my mom would just show up at my grandma's church and surprise her. If my grandma was at work, my mom used to just pop up with us at the restaurant my grandma worked and quietly sit at the counter. My grandma would come down to take our orders and realize it was her daughter and grandkids and she would have the biggest smile on her face and proudly introduce us to everyone that came into the restaurant. I remember us going to the hospital to see my mom. She was sitting up in this blue chair doing dailies and she looked around and said I'm not going to be able to go shopping anymore because I can't walk. We laughed so hard and told her we have to take her in a wheelchair. That's the thing about our mom. On her worst days, she finds a way to make you laugh or she will play her pain down.

For so long she didn't let us know how sick she was. All we knew was that she was back and forth to the doctor's appointments. She just kept pushing on through and tried to keep things as normal as possible. Weeks went by and we all hoped that one day, we will see her sharing her testimony and telling us how good God is.

The Call That
Changed Everything

October 5, 2001, it was about five in the morning. I woke up out of my sleep to the house phone ringing. I rushed to pick it up because my little sister was in bed with me, and I didn't want it to wake her up. Halfway asleep, I said hello and all I heard was my grandma on the phone yelling and crying… she's gone! She's gone! Ger here now!!! I called my sister and woke everyone up in the house. We all went to the hospital. We got to the hospital and so many people were there to say their goodbyes. Walking into that room, I said to myself, I cannot believe that the woman that went to the hospital so many times and came back as if nothing happened was dead.

That praying momma, that praying grandma, that praying aunt, that praying sister, that praying friend passed on. I think I can honestly speak for all my sisters and me. We thought this was going to be like all the other times she was gonna pull through and we would be out shopping somewhere, and she will be telling us her testimony. I saw myself going to her bedside so many times trying to tell her what had happened, but I couldn't. I just didn't have the strength or courage to tell her the shame and guilt. The embarrassment and the disappointment wouldn't allow me to tell her.

As I touched my mom's hand for the last time, I kept telling myself naw, she's a warrior, she's going to make it and maybe I'll tell her then. At the last minute, she was going to get up and it would be a miracle. But they got all of us in the room and explained to us that they were ready to unhook the machine and they had done all they could for her. The nurse came in and cut the machine off. We saw her take her last breath. Her chest went up and down and she was gone. I couldn't believe it. My mom, my everything was gone and at that moment our lives were instantly changed forever.

Passing of a Warrior

Lord, when my mom passed, it was like watching everyone's world fall apart, my grandma, my sisters, her grandkids, mom's brother, her father, her nieces and nephews. In fact, that day blew everyone's world up. Everyone who knew my mom knows she was crazy about her kids, grandkids, her nieces and nephews. She loved them as if she had given birth to them herself. As for her family, I have seen and heard her nieces and nephew talk about her and each time I see in their eyes and hear in their voices the same hurt and pain we feel to this day. I watched her brother look at my sister in disbelief as we all have something to remind him of his sister.

To this day, whenever my grandma talks about her daughter, her voice cracks and her eyes get so sad. My grandma buried her one and only daughter. She had to build her courage up and come back to her daughter's house and stay to make sure everyone was okay. When my mom first passed, every time my grandma talked about my mama, she would cry. She was so angry. Once my mom passed, my grandma told us that the doctor said they like to do a successful transplant, but my mom's case wouldn't be successful because, in the next couple of years, she will need another one.

I was mad for a long time at the doctor. Yes, my mom had a transplant in 1996 and in 2001 she needed another one. At this time, my mom's youngest biological child was seven and she had six other children. She had foster children that were about two and I think 10 or 11 years. She had grandkids, nieces and nephews who she loved dearly. She was a big sister, a daughter and a great friend. I didn't see how a doctor could not see how important she was. My mom helped any and everybody that she could, and she would always say God will bless me.

For a while I questioned God. How could they think that the life of a person that had done so much, had a good life and accomplished so much wasn't worth saving?

That was my last chance to tell her what they had done to me, and I still couldn't do it! After staying with her for some time, it was time to leave her. We all walked out of the room, our heads bowed and tears rolling. So many broken hearts quietly walked back to the waiting room and as we were making plans on what funeral home to go through, "he" said, I know a cheap funeral home. That waiting room went up in an uproar. We felt that the woman that had done so much for so many will be put away like the queen she was. She had been working hard and saving; she buried herself and paid for her own headstone.

My sisters and I went and picked out my mom's outfit and we went to Johnson- Miller Funeral home. A lady named Carrie, who was the funeral director, was nice and she helped us. I think she knew and saw it in our faces. We were young and didn't know what we were doing so she was patient and helped us. All the pastors at Monroe Church at the time stepped in and did what they could. The church had a repass set up after and they even made provision for a police escort to the gravesite. Little things like this mean a lot. When you think you have it all figured out and you're doing things by yourself, God puts his hand in the mix and reminds you that he always gives you what you need.

We picked her casket out and my sister's beautician, Willie did her hair with her signature finger waves. Johnson's funeral did a beautiful job with our mom. I was still in disbelief, and I didn't believe my mom passed even when we came to see her for the last time. She looked so peaceful like she had just come out of the church and was lying down taking a nap. In my head, I kept picturing her getting up and saying she was just playing. I know it sounds crazy but if you really know my mom, she will joke around. So, I kept waiting for her to get up with that beautiful smile.

I remember one year, for Christmas my mom tricked everyone. She gave all of us old coats and purses for Christmas, so everyone opened their gifts looking crazy and confused and she sat there watching us with that beautiful heavenly smile of hers. My mom never broke character. One of my sisters checked the pockets and started yelling check the pockets, there is money in the pockets and sure enough that big, beautiful smile came across her face and we all laughed so hard. She had put hundreds of dollars bills in the pockets of the coats and purses.

While standing there, all these different happy memories kept going through my head. I cannot remember one time in life she wasn't there, so now how do I move on? What do I do if she's not getting up? Still in disbelief as we left the viewing, somehow, I was still thinking that it was not real. Friends and family members were giving their condolences and I still couldn't believe it. We went back home to prepare for the funeral. That Friday, while getting ready for the funeral, I still didn't believe she was gone. We all scrambled around to get ready, and someone kept yelling the limo will be here soon and we had to be ready. It was literally like I was outside of my body watching everything. The ride to the church was so quiet, it looked like everything was going in slow motion.

The church was full so many pastors in the pulpit. We had a few pastors in our family and you know every last one of them spoke of the kind of person my momma was and how she was always praying and checking on people while she was going through her own challenges. The church was jam-packed with so many people she had touched in her 44 short years on this earth. People were in the choir stands, standing by the walls and every seat was full. People stood outside and they were trying to get in and say their goodbyes.

Watching her three brothers, two oldest nephews and her cousin carry her into the church for the last time and watching her nephews trying to stay strong was the most heartbreaking thing ever. Your heart just keeps breaking into what seems like a million pieces. My grandma was so heartbroken and sad. We were all so scared for her when we talked to her or saw her. We just learned to hold our tears back, listen and let her grieve for as long as she needed to. And then I looked up and saw the monster sitting up on the roll with my little sister. My stomach turned. Lord knows I just wanted to come from behind him and choke him to death.

I sat there thinking; why her and not him? It made me so mad and then the other person came and tried to look pitiful. When they said the casket would be open for the last time, I stood by the casket and still couldn't tell her it was my last chance. I could not tell her I felt so disappointed in myself. But I had to stop thinking about me and watch him and make sure he didn't try anything with my sister. I had to put my feelings away and go back to my seven-year-old sister as if nothing happened. I never let her see me crying. After my mom's funeral, she and I went downtown so I could get legal guardianship for her because I knew anytime, he wanted to he could come and take her.

We talked to the judge and the same day he gave us our guardianship papers and with that piece of paper I felt a little safer. I felt she was somehow protected, and he couldn't just come and take her. I kept telling myself, if he would ever try to come and take her, I would tell the judge what they had done to me. I love my sisters dearly and I would have given my life before I would let my sister be around that monster.

Moving on Without my Momma

My heart hurt so badly to the point that sometimes I felt like couldn't breathe. How do I move on without my momma? I have younger sisters looking up to me for guidance and I'm stuck because all I ever knew and loved was momma. My mom catered and sheltered me. If I had a problem, I would take it to her, and she would figure things out for me. I was the oldest still at home when my mom passed and just turned 25 on September 21. So, automatically, I was the head of a household with three sisters younger than me and my mom's business. I felt like I should never be vulnerable because people could try to use that against me.

I did what I always do, just kept my feelings to myself and tried to move the best way I know how. My sister and I already had everything we needed to run the daycare. My sister had been working with my mom full time for a couple of years up to the time she died, and I worked with them part-time when I didn't have to work at Value City. I just threw myself into work. We were open 24 hours long days and nights some overnights. I was in survival mode. My mom was gone, and we had to stay afloat.

It was always the fear of losing everything. If I knew what I know now, I would have taken some time off so we could just bond and learn how to move on without our mom. I should have gotten counseling for my sisters and should have been in counseling but at the time, black people were not talking or thinking about counseling. So, you just keep pushing yourself. I now know I made some mistakes along the way in parenting but when you become a parent, no one will give you a handbook. There is really no right and wrong way of parenting. I have now realized that you have to learn each child and be a parent based on the particular needs of the child and I would never do anything intentionally to hurt my family and I need to forgive myself.

Devil Shows up
at my Door

A couple of years after my mom passed, he became sick and was living a couple of blocks away from us with his nephew. One day he just popped up. I heard a knock at the front door. Looking out the window while standing there at that moment, my heart just dropped. What is he doing here? What does he want? I was scared and I went back to feeling like that little lost girl. I got my sister and took her to her room, closed the door and told her to stay there and I'll come back for her. I left him standing outside on the porch. My hands were shaking, my voice cracking.

I called my sister and told her that her father was here. She called his nephew he stayed with, and he came and got him. He apologized for his uncle coming over and said It wouldn't happen again and he never came back to the house after that. But for a while, I was back on edge. Some years later, some of his family reached out to me and asked if he ever did anything to me. I ran to the basement; my heart was beating so fast.

I was so scared and embarrassed and at first, I didn't say anything and then she said he had done something to someone else and they were trying to deal with it.

That call made me feel so dirty, ashamed, and embarrassed. And still, I could not come out and speak my entire truth and tell them the extent of the molestation and rape. I didn't say anything about the other person, I just said yes. The call was so weird, and we quietly hung up the phone. I was mad at his family because y'all knew he was a monster, and he was doing this and y'all watched him move in with a woman with little girls. We have to start speaking up and speaking out even if it's our fathers, uncles, brothers, sons, cousins, nephews who are doing these things. We have to make other people aware so they will not go through what we did. We cannot keep protecting these abusers! This is not our guilt, shame, embarrassment or fault and we shouldn't carry their wrongdoing.

Why Me

Oftentimes I tried to figure it out. I kept asking myself why me? Was it because I was my mom's darkest child? What made me so horrible of a kid that he chose me to be his victim? It made me dislike my skin color and I used to tell my sisters that when I have a baby, I'm going to have it by a white man so she can be light skinned with good hair. For so many years, I quietly struggled with my skin complexion because, in my head, I assumed that that was why he chose me. I never told anyone that I started self-harming myself.

My Greatest Gifts

On May 22, 2004, I had my first living child. I had been with her father for three years and we never talked about having kids together. I was on birth control and the last thing on my mind was having a baby. I had my little sister and all these nieces and nephews that were like my kids. I just woke up one morning sick. The flu was going around, and I honestly thought I had the flu. For a couple of days, I could not keep anything on my stomach. I just felt sick. A couple of my sisters were at the house, and I was lying in bed and one of them said, "You're pregnant," and I'm like no, I'm not. I have the flu. My period came every month and on time, so I just knew I wasn't pregnant.

That was the last thing on my mind. Knowing I had lost a baby before this relationship, and we never spoke of wanting to have kids. My sisters were like, take a pregnancy test. But I felt I wasn't prepared to waste my money on that bullshit because I just knew I wasn't pregnant. One of my sisters volunteered to get one from the store. She insisted that I should get up and take the test. I felt she just wasted her money, but I went into the bathroom and took the test. I came out and my sister waited for the result while I went back to bed.

Suddenly, I heard yelling and laughter; TAYE is pregnant. They were all running and screaming Taye is pregnant! Everyone was so excited. Her father and I went back and forth to the doctor more often than others because I was high risk. I had lost my first baby at six months with no warning. Everything was going on well until I was about 24 to 25 weeks when I had a doctor's appointment. They were checking me and discovered that I wasn't feeling any pain and I was amazed. I was having contractions and for some reason, I could not feel them.

Every time they stopped, and I move they will start again so they put me in the hospital for six weeks on strict bed rest. They just kept saying we need to get you to 32 weeks before they can deliver her. I laid in that bed for six weeks. I could not get up and go to the bathroom and I couldn't even get out of bed to sit in the chair next to the bed. I had to just lie there. Even though family and friends came and left, I kept saying that I wanted to go. I had to get back to work. Days and nights passed, different roommates came and left, and I was still there.

When I was about 30 weeks, they started preparing me. The doctor came in and said I would be getting a shot of steroids in two sets to help mature the baby's lungs. I called my sister and told her what they said. I was like they said I can go home and while I was getting ready, they came running back in and said we can't let you go. The baby's heart rate keeps dropping and we don't know why, so we are going to induce you. I talked to the doctor and nurse from the NICU (Newborn Intensive Care Unit). They were telling me the steps that will be taken after my baby is born.

I called my sister back and told her they said they were going to induce me. I was so scared and thought that it was happening again. I thought my baby was not going to make it. Lord, I needed my momma. I wanted that experience that my sisters had with her being in the delivery room with them and praying for them. I desired the experience of her bonding for the first time with my daughter. Two of my sisters and my daughter's father were in the delivery room and it was an easy birth.

I pushed once and the doctor said I see her head, push again and then he stopped me. I pushed for the third time, and she was here. A little white baby with jet black hair. The most beautiful baby I have ever seen. She could not stay in the room with me, they had to take her to the NICU. I was so scared she was not there with me. I thought, what if someone comes and steals my baby?

When my family came to see the baby, just as the team of doctors came through, that was how all my sisters, and their kids came through. I get embarrassed easily and because there are so many of us it would be loud. When I got there, I didn't see my baby out there with all the other babies and my heart dropped. I went in and talked to the nurse, and she said they had to put her in an incubator. One of my proudest moments was everyone coming to the window, and I went into the room to get her so they could see her. The nurse asked who they were, and I proudly said all six of them are my sisters and my nieces and nephews.

One of the saddest parts of having a baby is knowing that my child would not have a grandma or grandfather. I guess that was why God blessed me with so many sisters. God showed up once again and they kept my baby girl for only a week. I was so nervous about leaving my baby and my mind just went wild every day while my baby was in that hospital. I worked a little and went up there with my baby. The day I was able to bring her home was the proudest moment of my life. Things were going fine with her father and I until she was a year old.

Truth be told, he was just as broken as me and we had absolutely no business being together. A lot of disrespect was dished out and the first time I received that call, I should have been gone. But I stayed and four years later, we were still in this on and off relationship and I found out that I was pregnant. On Thanksgiving, we had dinner at my sister's house. My sister, her husband, a friend and I caught the Black Friday sale. My sister was at the register paying for the stuff she bought while I paid for mine. I walked to the bathroom because I started getting hot and I needed some water.

My friend and I went to the bathroom and suddenly everything went blank. All I could hear was her yelling Taye had just passed out. My sister came in and they got me back into the car. My friend called my sisters yelling that Taye had just passed out. I took a test, and I was pregnant. I didn't have a stomach; my menstrual cycle has always been off, but I still was coming on. First, I was shocked, then I started to worry like what am I going to do?

At this point, his father and I were on and off. I honestly didn't know how to tell him. He came to pick our daughter up and I put the pregnancy test in the diaper bag. May 12, 2008, I gave natural birth to a big red baby boy named Dajuan Keshaun Johnson. I had worked that day. I told my sister after the last kid left that I was going to the hospital. My leg has been hurting for a week. I didn't know what a contraction felt like because, with the first two, I couldn't feel contractions.

Once again, we have the waiting room full with all my sisters, their kids and my daughter. I could hear them while I was in my room. The nurse came in and looked at me and told me the doctor will be in to look at me and that he was going to send me home. But by this time the pain became unbearable. I had never felt pain like that before. My doctor came right in, looked at me and told me I had dilated to 6cm. I asked him if I could get the epidural and he told me no that it was too late. Two of my sisters, a friend and my son's father were in the room when I gave birth. I was in so much painful that I could not understand absolutely anything.

I never felt pain like this before. I wish my mom was here. I needed her now more than ever. After all that pain, God blessed me with a big red healthy handsome baby boy.

When it comes to having kids, my stress level often went to an all-time high. No one could understand why I couldn't let my kids spend the night somewhere. Everyone will get offended, but they will not understand why I would have to call or text them all the time when I let my kids go somewhere. Are y'all okay? Did anything happening? It's very important to me that I ask all the necessary questions when they go somewhere or when I go somewhere. How are you doing? Any problems, who are the people there and how do they make you feel. As with my mom, she did all the other things except ask such questions. She thought that since this was family the questions weren't necessary.

The Devil Returned
To Hell

I can't remember who told me he had died. I was so happy because for so long I had questioned God and kept asking why? I couldn't understand why he allowed my mom to suffer so much and take her from us knowing we still needed her. My youngest sister was only seven. She really never had the time to bond with her because she was sick all her life. Why would he do that? But letting a monster live and giving him more years than my mom; I couldn't say anything now. How will I ever tell them now that their father had died? I wouldn't dare to hurt my sisters anymore.

They lost my mom and now their father. My Lil sister was in high school when he died. I had to be strong for her. Preparing to go to his funeral, I literally had to talk myself into going. I knew I had to be there for my sisters and also, I had to make sure the devil went back to hell. I knew if I didn't go, I would have to explain to them why. Once I walked through that door, even though he was dead, it was like I was back in his presence again as fear took over me. I was so scared as I quietly walked to the middle of the church pew with my sisters.

I tried to keep my head down and I sat there so scared. I felt so small while sitting there and it was like I was having an out-of-body experience. I saw my sisters going around the casket. I saw them sad and that made me sad as well. On one side I thought of all the horrible things this man had done to me and on the other hand, I was also sad because my sisters lost their father, and they didn't experience him as I did.

I was mad at myself because I was sad for the person who caused me all this pain. Although I thought maybe something was wrong with me because the other side of me was happy, perhaps the reason was that I knew he was gone and could never hurt me again. His son walked over and spoke to us, and my blood just started boiling. How dare you come and speak as if you have done nothing. Over the years, I only saw him every now and then when my sisters used to invite him to things they had. I tried my best to stay as far as possible from him and to keep my Lil sister away but now he is before us.

In my mind, I could visualize myself getting up and choking the shit out of him. I remember how mad I used to be at my sisters when they bragged about their brother... my brother this, my brother that. I wanted to tell them so badly man fuck your brother, he ain't shit just like his daddy but I won't dare. I just swallowed my pride and kept quiet. They finally did the last viewing of the body and closed the casket forever. Yes! The devil is finally locked in hell forever and he can no longer hurt anyone. As the funeral service was ending and my sisters prepared to go to the burial and the repass, I went home. I will not watch his family tell lies like he was so good. Nope, I went home and got myself together so that when my sisters came back home, I can be there for them.

Willing to Accept
Almost Anything

I was willing to accept almost anything so my kids would never have to feel abandoned like I did as a child because my father was not there or experience the things I did as child I was totally against having anyone besides my kids' father around them. My family could not understand why but I knew why I allowed the mistreatment I was willing to sacrifice my happiness for my kids. The truth is the first time he cheated I should have been gone. But he was my kids' father he was the first man that told me love me. But deep down I knew this wasn't love love does not feel like that.   The disrespect just got worst female calling my phone, taken my kids around females he's in relationship with while still with me, cheating with someone that stayed   around the corner from sister and so much more. I remember having my first big break down   after taking years of the cheating verbal abuse   my sister, a friend and I were sitting in my backyard. They were on the porch while I was sitting in a chair facing the opposite direction and tears just started rolling down my face.

I couldn't control them anymore. I was sitting there and quietly falling apart. I was so broken; I didn't know what to do or what to think. All I kept thinking of was how I had fucked up my kids' life. Thirteen years of my life gone, and I allowed this man to disrespect me for so long. So scared of the outside world and scared to walk away from what I knew. My Daughter came over to the chair and started yelling "Tete my mom "ALLJESUS" (allergies) acting up!

We laughed so hard, and it was like that was all I needed. I knew my daughter was watching me and I had to do better for her and her brother. I was so hurt but I wasn't mad – just DONE. I watched this man drag my name through the mud and I just kept saying God knows the truth. He would tell anyone that would listen how I kept him from his kids. But the two of us and God know why and I'm just going to leave it at that.

I cut off all communication with him and if it wasn't anything important about my kids, I didn't talk to him at all. My kids were at the age where they could communicate well with him; they had their own phones. He didn't like that at all. The verbal abuse got really bad when I started setting boundaries, so I had to block his number. This man had done so much low-down shit to me that he couldn't take it After 13 years of bull shit, I was done. He tried to run the guilt trip on me but for me, it was over, and I was never ever going back.

He said, "ain't nobody gone to want you, you have two kids!" I really didn't care because, at that point, I had already vowed not to date till my kids were older. I know for a fact that if I didn't have the courage and strength to walk away, this would've still been going on. I thank God all the time for the strength courage and peace he gave me to leave that situation. The first couple of holidays were hard but God and my family got me through. I remember the first Valentine's Day, I wasn't going to get my hair done and my sisters were like, girl go get your hair done and celebrate yourself.

I went. Her and my youngest sister were all dressed up with our red on and the end up being one of best Valentine's Day that I can remember after the breakup. I remember one of my sisters calling me and saying, until you get a boyfriend, I'll be your boyfriend. One of my sister's boyfriends bought me some flowers and balloons. My kids made me cards at that moment. I knew what it meant when they say God will give you what you need. I was at my lowest and I could barely look at my kids without hurting. All the holidays we spent together for so many years were no more. But God!

To my Kids' Father

I am forever grateful to you. You blessed me with Daniya and Dajuan and if I had to go through that hell to get to them, I would without a shadow of doubt. I can't keep blaming you for the things I allowed you to do to me. I have to take accountability and some responsibility. You only did what I allowed you to do. For so long I was mad at you because you knew me like no other. You knew I wasn't going to leave; you knew I was never going to cheat back; you knew all I had been through.

You knew I was totally against someone else around my kids because of the things I have been through with my stepfather and brother, and you took advantage of that. But now I thank God for putting forgiveness in my heart and I can truly say I accept your apology. I know that I deserve better I'm worthy of love, someone is going to love my kids as their own All men are not the same, I do wish you joy, happiness, good health and love. Know that I have found peace with the situation and wish you nothing but happiness.

A Letter to my Father

I'm not sure what to call you. Do I call you dad, daddy or Jerome? If you were in my life, I often wonder what I would have called you. But since you weren't and I don't feel right calling you dad or daddy for now, I'm just going to settle and call you Jerome.

Dear Jerome, why did you leave? Why weren't you there? Why didn't you love me? Was I not beautiful enough to love? Was I not important enough for you to check in on me often? What did I ever do to you that made you not want me? Mom has gotten her wings and I can't ask her. She has never said one negative word about you, so I need to hear from you why? I was never able to understand or wrap my mind around how someone would have kids and not give a fuck about them. How do you continue moving on with your life? You don't know if your child has eaten, if they are safe or if they have a roof over their head. Because as a parent, I can never imagine being in this world and just moving on as if my kids don't matter.

I tried to put myself in your shoes and I can't understand it. I know God said we should not judge and I'm honestly trying not to judge but why weren't you there? Why is my mom not mad? She used to always tell me with that beautiful smile she would often say Taye, you have to forgive him not for him but for you. When you're young, you really don't know the meaning of that. I do wish you were there when I was younger. Often, I would picture you coming into the fire and pulling me out of hell. I waited so many years for you, but you never came. I often wonder if you were involved in my life, would I feel proactive and safe to tell you about the molestation and rape?

If I had told you, would you have stepped in to save me? When your sister passed and my sister daughter and I came to Poochie funeral, do you know how it felt trying to grieve for our aunt while being an outcast? Grown people looked at us like we didn't belong. Did you know we had a close lovely relationship with your sister and for as long as we could remember, she has always been there? Did you know that even though you didn't man up and claim us, your sister did? Did you know your sister and I had many disagreements about you? Did you know that before she passed, we had been in talk, and she planned to come up here and spend some time with us?

Did you know after mom passed that she still stayed in contact with us and checked in with us? Do you know how it feels to be in the same room as your birth father and he has to be forced to come over and speak to his kids and granddaughter? There were so many birthdays, graduations, baby showers, kids' birth and deaths that I needed your shoulder to cry on and you weren't there. I do forgive as God has forgiven me for the wrongs I have done. But I am determined to break this cycle as I guide my kids through their journey.

I don't want them thinking like I did and thinking that because a parent is not there they are less. I don't want them to feel unwanted and unloved because a parent is too selfish and doesn't want to take responsibility and accountability for not being there. I have now come to terms with the situation, and I now accept things for what they are. I am no longer mad and bitter about you not being there. I wish you so much love, happiness and blessing. I forgive you.

Playlist that got me through writing this book

1. Donald Lawrence feat. Le'Andria Johnson - Deliver me (This is my Exodus)

2. Tasha Cobbs - Break every chain, You know my name

3. Hezekiah Walker - God Favored me

4. Yolanda Adams - The Battle Is not Yours, Be Blessed

5. Le'Andria Johnson - Better Days

6. Smokie Norful - I Need You now

7. Tamela Mann - Take me to the King

8. Travis Green - Made A Way

9. The Rance Allen Group feat. Kirk Franklin - Something About The Name Jesus

10. Georgia Mass Choir - Come On In The Room

11. William Becton & Friends Be Encouraged

12. Greg O'Quin & Joyful Noize - I Told the Storm

13. Marvin Sapp - Never would've made it

14. The Williams Brothers - Still Here

15. Kory Hawthorne - Won't He Do It

16. Mary Mary - Go Get It, Can't Give Up Now, Shackles, Yesterday

17. Mary J Blige - Just Fine, No More Drama

18. Beyonce - Me Myself And I

19. India Arie - Steady Love And Brown Skin

20. Fantisha - Lose To Win, Free Yourself, Ain't Gon' Beg You, Baby Mama

21. Jordan Spark - One Wing

22. Uncle Sam - I Don't Ever Want To See You Again

23. Keyshia Cole - I Remember, I Should've cheated, Trust And Believe

24. Syleena Johnson - Guess What

25. Tamia- Stranger - In My House

26. Monica - Still Standing

27. YG - My Hitta

And so many more. Music is powerful and it can help you in your darkest hours when you don't have the words to say.

Learning to stand in my truth

About the Author

As embarrassing and ugly as my truth is, I now stand in it at the age of 44 with my head held high. I now know that telling my truth and standing in my truth is not to make anyone else feel bad and it is not dishonoring my momma. But it is for me to heal and move on with my life and maybe I can help someone in the process and finally have a chance at truly being  happy and open to love. I had so much rage and I didn't trust anyone. I was so aggressive and guarded.

I'm forever grateful to God for my sisters, grandma and real friends that saw me breaking and had that hard talk with me. I am also grateful to God for the ones that knew my heart and were able to deal with my guarded and standoffish ways. I'm so, so, so thankful. I'm thankful he chose my kids as mine to make me want to do and be a better woman, stand up for myself, take some accountability and control of my life.

I'm thankful to my nieces and nephews. Some of y'all were like my first kids and y'all opened me up to love and hugs. I'm forever grateful for my mom who was a praying woman and introduced me to God at a young age because if I didn't know or have faith in God, I don't know if I would have been able to make it this far.

No, I'm not a pastor, evangelist, or a motivational speaker. I am brave, I am worthy, I am beautiful, I am a survivor and a child of God. What I do have is courage, faith, God, my kids and my family. I am standing in my truth; I am a single woman at the age of 44 and that's nothing to be ashamed of. I am learning to love myself more and more every day. I now know my purpose and I am a child of God. To anyone that has gone or is going through or a similar experience, understand that it is not your fault. So please SPEAK UP, SPEAK OUT!! Only you can tell your story.

Contact Daphne @ johnsondaphne@ymail.com

Interested In Writing & Or Publishing a Book
Visit Dr. Synovia @a2zbookspublishing.net